THE AMERICAN STIMULUS PROGRAM

Empowering Citizens to Create Economic Stimulus Every Week

MICHAEL PALSER

ISBN- 9798702018171

Contents

Dedication

This book is devoted to the members of Congress that step forward to help embrace and endorse a genuinely nonpartisan bill. This book is committed to the President of the United States, who will sign that bill into law. This book is dedicated to all of those who participate in the American Stimulus Program. Together we can unleash economic prosperity created *by* and *for* the people of the United States of America!

<u>What is the American Stimulus Program?</u>

We can take a small sliver of our disposable income and funnel it together to stimulate and strengthen our economy's most vital component: consumer spending. The American Stimulus Program will put cold hard cash into the hands of hundreds of thousands of Americans each week! It will work for all fifty states, no matter what their current economic circumstances may be. The ASP is not a new tax or entitlement program. It is not a lottery. It does not eliminate any federal programs that currently exist. It is an unbiased, nonpartisan, economic tool, unlike the world has ever seen.

As we look toward our future, America has been through an awful lot. The coronavirus blindsided us. We agreed to a voluntary shutdown of our country to slow the spread of Covid-19. We witnessed George Floyd's death, followed by various protests, demonstrations, riots, and looting. Unemployment reached record levels. In response, the Federal Government started a series of stimulus programs to help us pay our bills, support our businesses, and keep us safe. All of this happened as we approached the 2020 Presidential election, exposing a very divided country.

Coronavirus has claimed over 400,000 American lives so far. The economic fallout has also been extensive, resulting in lost jobs, lost businesses, and lost hope. Luckily, we are slowly learning how to manage Covid-19 and reduce the staggering death toll. We are finding our way past the coronavirus, but the America we knew will not be the same for the foreseeable future.

Our experiences associated with work, school, socializing, recreation, and relationships can be challenging. We are struggling to regain our balance in the pursuit of our ambitions and dreams. It is also apparent that federal stimulus packages, emergency business loans, extended unemployment benefits, and government handouts cannot continue indefinitely.

The Federal Government's first stimulus package totaling over five trillion dollars took them nearly five years to collect through taxation. This continued artificial injection of currency into our economy will inevitably result in higher taxes, more regulations, and less buying power for each dollar that we earn. We need a new approach. We need the American Stimulus Program!

The ASP has only three functions. First, it distributes cash prizes every seven days that match our national median weekly earnings. It provides money for our immediate use and will help to stimulate consumer spending. It can help us to restart the critical chain of developers, manufacturers, distributors, and retailers. This Program will grease the wheel of capitalism and help keep consumer spending healthy during any economic cycle.

Secondly, the American Stimulus Program will help to replenish our state and local tax bases. Covid-19 has created huge deficits in each state. To put it nicely, our state governments are, for the most part, broke. We need money to fight the virus, but we also need funds to run our cities and towns and all the necessary services that they provide. Every state would welcome the consistent influx of weekly state and local tax revenue, and the ASP can give it. And significant dollars at that.

And finally, the American Stimulus Program can provide tax revenue for the Federal Government. We all fear that they will raise taxes soon to make up for the monstrous deficits we face due to Covid-19. The ASP will allow Americans to effectively participate in a program to impede and discourage new taxes. We can lift ourselves up and catapult our economy back to where it was and help it grow. It will help millions who are drowning in worry and debt. It is simple, transparent, powerful, and fun!

A Big Idea Financed by Spare Change

Consumer spending creates sixty to seventy percent of our economic stability in the United States. On average, Americans consume more than 400 million cups of coffee at an estimated cost of 1.2 billion dollars per day. Per day! Imagine how much money we collectively spend on groceries, fast food, entertainment, plus all those impulse buys we make daily. Consumer spending is the real bread and butter of the American economy.

The old saying is, "everything starts with a sale." Simple transactions like buying coffee support a long chain of related businesses. Our economy relies on consumer demand to gauge the allocation and distribution of economic resources. When consumer spending increases, our economic indicators turn positive, resulting in financial strength, business expansion, and new jobs.

Unfortunately, cycles of growth are inevitably interrupted by temporary economic declines known as recessions. These are periods of intermittent economic downswing where trade and production decrease at an alarming rate. The money simply dries up for one reason or another. Since 1945, the United States has experienced twelve different recessions. Fortunately, they have only lasted on average about eleven months. In between recessionary periods, we have encountered nearly six years of expansion and growth. Currently, we are experiencing the elements of a recession triggered by a worldwide pandemic.

We seem to be helpless to stop the decrease of economic damage when a recession does occur. We need a financial tool to ensure consistent consumer spending, infuse federal and state tax bases, reduce taxation, and strengthen our economy. What if the money to drive America's economy did not dry up during economic declines? What if there was a constant influx of currency to the American people that was not an artificial stimulus created by the Federal Government? How could we do that, and what would it look like?

The American Stimulus Program allows us to invest in ourselves to help ourselves! We could take some of our spare change to strengthen our economy. We could pool these funds and redistribute them amongst ourselves to keep consumer spending healthy and consistent. We have discovered that new stimulus is the fastest, most efficient, and useful tool to get our economy back on track. We could do this as effortlessly as downloading a computer app on our smartphones or streaming devices.

This Program will create statewide stimulus pools to distribute cash prizes to hundreds of thousands of Americans every week! The American Stimulus Program will also withhold taxes for all winning citizens. If you have won $1000 this week, you have genuinely won around $1400 before taxes. But why be burdened with tax withholdings? The ASP removes the taxes, and when you see $1000 posted to your account, that is your money! That is cash created by Americans investing in themselves. And when you decide to spend it, you will be investing in the United States economy while making that money work for you.

We are at a critical time in our country's history. Americans need cash now more than ever. In addition to our current chronic unemployment problem, we have bills and lots of debt. Debt! Rent, mortgages, alimony, child support, medical bills, credit card bills, student loans, personal loans, phone bills, utility bills, auto loans, and payday loans weigh heavily on many Americans.

The American Stimulus Program will help alleviate the pressure of our money worries during rough recessionary periods and in times of recovery and expansion. Just keep in mind that we are fueling our economic engine every time we spend money in America. It all counts!

Job Earnings Created in The Aggregate

Aggregate: A whole formed by combining many separate elements or items.

There is an inspirational sports film called "Moneyball." It documents the 2002 baseball season of the Oakland Athletics. In the movie, General Manager Billy Beane and assistant GM Peter Brand take on building a competitive major league baseball team with a limited budget. They agreed to develop their team by utilizing sabermetrics. They applied statistical analysis to compare individual players' performance and selected talent based on their unique yet unrecognized skillset. The A's were unable to sign top tier talent due to their money constraints, but their system uncovered quality undervalued players. It allowed them to sign talent for pennies on the dollar. In theory, they could create a championship-caliber team in the aggregate. And it worked!

The A's finished first in the American League West with an impressive 103 wins and 59 losses. They also won 20 consecutive games setting a record at the time. Even more impressive was that A's management had found a way to spend only $260,000 for each win while the New York Yankees spent 1.4 million per triumph. The Yankees also won 103 games that season but at a whopping expense of $1,140,000 more per victory than the Oakland Athletics had paid!

The A's management set an excellent example of achieving a goal by putting together many undervalued assets to succeed. They did not have the money to sign Major League All-Stars, but they did find a pool of acute talent to play superior baseball on a shoestring budget. We can do the same thing to rebuild our economy.

We are currently missing millions of jobs and the necessary buying power that accompanies those jobs. Our unemployed workforce in the United States now lacks income, severely limiting consumer spending. Our economy has become restricted in its capacity to perform at an optimal level. We are experiencing an economy that is not working efficiently.

Americans need to earn to succeed. We are now facing the primary factor of recession: unemployment. So, let us take a page from the A's playbook and rebuild those lost wages in the aggregate. We can create a collective driven stimulus solution. We live in a time of technological wonder. The internet, smartphones, streaming devices, computer apps, electronic commerce, and digital banking are the tools we can utilize to rebuild our economy.

America is the most generous nation. We like to help whenever we can. Community collections, social media fundraisers, fund-me pages, charitable apps, and traditional charity drives help alleviate financial burdens created from tragedies or challenging circumstances each day. We all understand the importance of giving to help others. *Kindness may turn out to be the most powerful force of all.* Millions of Americans donate and invest billions of dollars to a myriad of benevolent causes. The American Stimulus Program allows us to help others as well as ourselves. For the first time in our nation's history, what if we could invest in our country, our economy, our home state, our hometowns, our fellow citizens, our families, and ultimately, ourselves? I am introducing an economic tool that rewards the charitable in return both quickly and efficiently!

The ASP can produce billions of dollars to substitute for lost earnings. The Program is a mix of investment, charity, and capitalism. This tool creates a unique balance of distributing disposable income directly to the people of our respective states while also providing the opportunity of enriching ourselves!

<u>Nuts & Bolts</u>

I have created the American Stimulus Program to inspire legislators to construct a national online infrastructure to help support the United States' citizens and our economy. Let us imagine that both the House of Representatives and the Senate have approved it. Let us also envision that our President has signed it into law. Soon after that, the ASP will be open for business. Here is how it works.

Signing up will be relatively simple. You will need to be at least 18 years of age to participate. You will be able to download the ASP computer application to your phone or streaming device. You can fill out your registration information, which will include your name, birth date, residence, social security number, bank account, and routing information for the immediate digital deposit of monies won. Upon completion, you will then have the option to buy tickets, priced at $5 each, for your state's weekly drawing. No credit card purchases will be allowed. This Program will not place any further credit debt on any American.

Each citizen may purchase up to 10 tickets for each weekly drawing. $50 is the most any American can invest each week. There are two reasons for the limit on tickets. First and foremost, this is a proactive economic program that will shield those susceptible to compulsive or excessive ticket purchasing. The second reason is to protect the integrity of the drawing. The limitation on individual ticket purchases provides a safeguard against large syndicates or investment groups from purchasing huge blocks of tickets to manipulate state drawings.

Let us say that you decide to purchase two tickets for $10, and you are a resident of Florida. Upon purchase, you will receive your tickets electronically. You will notice your Postal code, FL, followed by your ticket number. FL-24 translates to the 24th ticket purchased by a Floridian.

It is important to note here that states do not compete against one another for ASP dollars. It is not fair to pool the five-hundred and eighty-five thousand Wyoming citizens with the thirty-nine million people living in California. *Every state will have a drawing based on the monies pooled in that state and paid to the citizens of that state.*

Currently, the real median income in the United States is around $68,000. Depending upon your state and personal tax information, an employee earning 68K per year will take home roughly $1000 per week after taxes. Money won through the ASP is designed to emulate our actual average weekly job earnings. This Program will not produce retirement size jackpots. It will reward as many citizens as possible with cash prizes that reflect our current living cost and our weekly medium-income earnings. Using those weekly earnings as our guidepost, the American Stimulus Program can distribute over 460,000 prizes of $1000 each week. That is $460,000,000, paid directly back to us every seven days! The ASP provides an immediate fiscal stimulus that we can create ourselves weekly!

With hundreds of thousands of Americans winning $1000 each week, the ASP is essentially distributing funds just like a major corporation would pay its weekly payroll. However, unlike a traditional corporation, the ASP can exist in every urban, suburban, and rural community in the United States. Every American can participate. Each state would be creating its stimulus program. Weekly winners would be making an income equal to working a 40-hour workweek at $25 an hour after taxes. Nearly half a million people would be receiving money each week as though they received a $1000 bonus! The significance of the purchasing power that it will provide to the American people will be noteworthy in any economic cycle. Any questions?

How many people will most likely invest in the American Stimulus Program each week?

I have determined this by recognizing what I call "engaged citizens." Those are Americans who would most likely be involved in the ASP because they have a track record of participating in another nationwide voluntary event: our Presidential elections. In 2016, approximately 130 million people voted in the election. That represents almost 40% of our entire U.S. population. Amazingly, nearly 160 million voters participated in the 2020 election! Through that election process, we discovered an unintended consequence of the pandemic. We found out that by supplying a reasonable alternative to standing in line to vote to help reduce our population's exposure to the virus, mail-in ballots increased voter participation dramatically. I wonder how many more Americans would have voted if they could have done so online? We have learned that when we make it more convenient for the American people to participate in our national concerns, they will most definitely get involved!

Over 260 million Americans currently have smartphones, and over 97% of our population has access to the internet. According to CareerBuilder, nearly 78% of the U.S. workforce are living from paycheck to paycheck. Millions of Americans are on edge as their lack of employment and dwindling savings jeopardize their way of life. They require assistance while Congress determines the next stimulus alternative. The ASP will offer a simple and easy way for Americans to invest in themselves. They will have the means to create an income stream *by* and *for* the American people. It will only cost $5 per ticket or $0.72, set aside per day, to participate for an opportunity to win $1000 each week. The ASP will reach out and connect with as many people as it can. In the end, everyone can genuinely prosper both directly and indirectly. Whether you hold a winning ticket this week or not, our collective participation will increase consumer spending and raise tax dollars for our common good. We will be rebuilding our economy together. With those factors in mind, I will use half the number of voters who participated in each state during the 2016 Presidential election to estimate nationwide participation.

How much will the American Stimulus Program cost taxpayers to build?

In August 2014, a report was released by the Office of Inspector General, finding that the Healthcare.gov website cost approximately 1.7 billion. The ASP is essentially an online marketplace, a random ticket drawing program, and a digital cash distribution website for all fifty states. The construction is much simpler and more streamlined than our current online healthcare website. However, let us estimate using the worst-case price scenario and say it cost nearly 1.7 billion dollars. With roughly 20% of the U.S. population participating and producing an annual Federal Tax revenue of over 8.5 billion, the American Stimulus Program will quickly pay for itself in mere months!

How will the Federal taxes be determined?

Currently, there is a 24% flat tax on money won in the United States. Although all ASP tickets will not be winners, this is a federal program with three main objectives: stimulate consumer spending, produce state and local dollars, and create federal tax revenue. Keeping in line with the flat federal winning tax, a 24% ASP tax on each ticket will help pay for the Program itself and achieve the Federal revenue objective.

How will State Taxes be determined?

Combining the state and local sales tax rates in each state and applying it to each ticket purchase will determine state taxes. For example, in Florida, the state sales tax is 6%, the local sales tax rate is 1.05%, producing a combined rate of 7.05%. Therefore, in Florida, a $5 ticket will withhold $1.20 or 24% for Federal taxes and about $0.35 or 7.05% for state and local taxes. The ASP will take the $3.45 remaining and add it to the Florida Citizens Prize Pool for the weekly drawing. States without sales taxes may consider an excise tax to profit from the sale of American Stimulus Program tickets in those states.

Now, let us say that you tune in to watch the weekly drawing, and you are alerted that you possess a winning ticket. In Florida, your winning ticket is worth $1450.33. After taxes, you have won $1000 for your $5 investment! Congratulations, the ASP will immediately deposit one thousand dollars to your account!

The American Stimulus Program is not a lottery but a simple series of state-bound drawings. In 2018, if you combine both major lotteries in the United States, there were only 12 winning tickets! 12! Only 12 tickets won over 5 billion dollars! Furthermore, instead of the typical lottery odds of 292,000,000 to 1, the American Stimulus Program drawings offer odds on average of 288 to 1! For the lottery, Americans stand in long lines against impossible odds to put up hard-earned money they will surely lose. With this Program, there are no lines to purchase tickets. There is no number of combinations to select. There are only weekly state drawings to enrich Americans. Other than the taxes withheld, the ASP will pay 100% of the remaining funds to hundreds of thousands of Americans each week!

The American Stimulus Program Simulation
State by State

Each Sunday, the ASP will execute random drawings from all the tickets purchased in each state. The Citizens Prize Pool of each state will be divided by $1000 and will draw tickets until no prize pool money remains. In those instances when less than $1000 remains in the Citizens Prize Pool, the ASP will draw a single "mini prize" to exhaust all funds. Estimating how many tickets on average any individual American will purchase each week is difficult to predict. Americans may buy one ticket at $5 or up to ten tickets at $50. For this simulation, each participant's average purchase is $10 or 2 tickets. Every state has been included based on the parameters outlined in the previous chapter. Also added are yearly projections based on the weekly sample. Here are the results for each state.

ALABAMA – "The Heart of Dixie"
Odds of Winning in Alabama 300 to 1

WEEKLY DRAWING BASED ON AVERAGE PURCHASE OF $10 (2 TICKETS)
Participants: 1,061,686 or 21.7% of the State Population
State Pool: $10,616,860
State & Local Combined Sales Tax (9.22%): $978,874
Federal ASP Tax (24%): $2,548,046
Citizens Prize Pool: $7,089,940
WEEKLY DRAWING RESULTS: 7,089 Prizes of $1000 + 1 Mini Prize of $940

1 YEAR PROJECTION: BASED ON AVERAGE PURCHASE OF $10 (2 TICKETS)
Alabama Annual Revenue: $552,076,720
Alabama Annual Tax Revenue: $50,901,448
Annual Federal Tax Revenue: $132,498,392
Annual Winning Tickets of $1000 in Alabama: **368,628**
CASH PAID YEARLY TO ALABAMANS AFTER TAXES: $368,676,880

SWEET HOME ALABAMA!

That is some significant cash! Winning tickets awarded to the people of Alabama would be the equivalent of every man, woman, and child of Trussville (population 25,528), Fairhope (23,527), Pelham (24,334), Homewood (25,141), Northport (26,029), Bessemer (26,348), Athens (27,103), Daphne (23,378), Enterprise (28,979), Opelika (31,455), Alabaster (33,818), Vestavia Hills (34,411), Muscle Shoals (14,655), and Troy (population 18,930), **_all_ winning one-thousand dollars each after taxes!** And that is with only 21.7% of the state's population participating. The American Stimulus Program can add over **$400,000,000** to the economy of Alabama each year! Roll Tide!

ALASKA – "The Final Frontier"

Odds of Winning in Alaska 269 to 1

WEEKLY DRAWING BASED ON AVERAGE PURCHASE OF $10 (2 TICKETS)

Participants: 159,304 or 21.7% of the State Population
State Pool: $1,593,040
State & Local Combined Sales Tax (1.76%): $28,037
Federal ASP Tax (24%): $382,329
Citizens Prize Pool: $1,182,674
WEEKLY DRAWING RESULTS: 1,182 Prizes of $1000 + 1 Mini Prize of $674

1 YEAR PROJECTION: AVERAGE PURCHASE OF $10 (2 TICKETS)

Alaska Annual Revenue: $82,838,080
Alaska Annual Tax Revenue: $1,457,924
Annual Federal Tax Revenue: $19,881,108
Annual Winning Tickets of $1000 in Alaska: **61,464**
CASH PAID YEARLY TO ALASKANS AFTER TAXES: $61,499,048

NORTH TO ALASKA!

Winning tickets awarded to the people of Alaska would be the equivalent of every man, woman, and child of Anchor Point (population 2,093), North Pole (2,094), Willow (2,126), Cordova (2,169), Dillingham (2,360), Houston (2,412), Wrangell (2,502), Deltana (2,613), Ridgeway (2,617), Big Lake (2,765), Seward (2,796), Petersburg (3,106), Valdez (3,855), Nome (3,870), Butte (3,929), Goldstream (4,389), Unalaska (4,432), Sterling (5,321), and Farmers Loop (population 5,535) **_all_ winning one-thousand dollars each after taxes!** And that is with only 21.7% of the state's population participating. The American Stimulus Program can add over **$60,000,000** to the economy of Alaska each year! North to the future!

ARIZONA – "The Grand Canyon State"

Odds of Winning in Arizona 296 to 1

WEEKLY DRAWING BASED ON AVERAGE PURCHASE OF $10 (2 TICKETS)

Participants: 1,286,582 or 17.7% of the State Population
State Pool: $12,865,820
State & Local Combined Sales Tax (8.40%): $1,080,728
Federal ASP Tax (24%): $3,087,796
Citizens Prize Pool: $8,697,296
WEEKLY DRAWING RESULTS: 8,697 Prizes of $1000 + 1 Mini Prize of $296

1 YEAR PROJECTION: AVERAGE PURCHASE OF $10 (2 TICKETS)

Arizona Annual Revenue $669,022,640
Arizona Tax Revenue: $56,197,856
Federal Tax Revenue: $160,565,392
Annual Winning Tickets of $1000 in Arizona: **452,244**
CASH PAID YEARLY TO ARIZONIANS AFTER TAXES $452,259,392

ARIZONA GREEN!

Winning tickets awarded to the people of Arizona would be the equivalent of every man, woman, and child of Glendale (population 252,114), Yuma (98,285), San Tan Valley (93,230), Avondale (87,931), Goodyear (86,840), Buckeye (79,620), Flagstaff (75,038), Casas Adobes (69,615), Casa Grande (58,632), and Lake Havasu City (population 55,865) _**all**_ **winning one-thousand dollars each after taxes!** And that is with only 17.7% of the state's population contributing. The American Stimulus Program can add over **$500,000,000** to the economy of Arizona each year!

ARKANSAS – "The Natural State"

Odds of Winning in Arkansas 301 to 1

<u>**WEEKLY DRAWING BASED ON AVERAGE PURCHASE OF $10 (2 TICKETS)**</u>
Participants: 565,317 or 18.7% of the State Population
State Pool: $5,653,170
State & Local Combined Sales Tax (9.47%): $535,355
Federal ASP Tax (24%): $1,356,760
Citizens Prize Pool: $3,761,055
WEEKLY DRAWING RESULTS: 3761 Prizes of $1000 + 1 Mini Prize of $55

<u>**1 YEAR PROJECTION: AVERAGE PURCHASE OF $10 (2 TICKETS)**</u>
Arkansas Annual Revenue: $293,964,840
Arkansas Annual Tax Revenue: $27,838,460
Annual Federal Tax Revenue: $70,551,520
Annual Winning Tickets of $1000 in Arkansas: **195,572**
CASH PAID YEARLY TO ARKANSANS AFTER TAXES: $195,574,860

<u>**ALL GET OUT!**</u>
    Winning tickets awarded to the people of Arkansas would be the equivalent of every man, woman, and child of Texarkana (population 30,002), Bella Vista (28,999), Jacksonville (27,993), Cabot (27,147), West Memphis (23,996), El Dorado (17,600), Mountain Home (12,531), Lowell (9,968), Hope (9,541), and Trumann (population 7,101) *__all__* **winning one-thousand dollars each after taxes!** And that is with only 18.7% of the state's population contributing. The American Stimulus Program can add over **$200,000,000** to the economy of Arkansas each year!

CALIFORNIA – "The Golden State"

Odds of Winning in California 297 to 1

<u>WEEKLY DRAWING BASED ON AVERAGE PURCHASE OF $10 (2 TICKETS)</u>
Participants: 7,090,797 or 17.9% of the State Population
State Pool: $70,907,970
State & Local Combined Sales Tax (8.66%): $6,140,630
Federal ASP Tax (24%): $17,017,912
Citizens Prize Pool: $47,749,428
WEEKLY DRAWING RESULTS: 47,749 Prizes of $1000 + 1 Mini Prize of $428

<u>1 YEAR PROJECTION: AVERAGE PURCHASE OF $10 (2 TICKETS)</u>
California Annual Revenue: $3,687,214,440
California Annual Tax Revenue: $319,312,760
Annual Federal Tax Revenue: $884,931,424
Annual Winning Tickets of $1000 in California: **2,482,948**
CASH PAID YEARLY TO CALIFORNIANS AFTER TAXES: $2,482,970,256

<u>GET STOKED!</u>

    Winning tickets awarded to the people of California would be the equivalent of every man, woman, and child of San Francisco (population 881,549), Sacramento (513,624), Anaheim (350,365), Pasadena (141,029), Santa Clara (130,365), Berkeley (121,363), East Los Angeles (119,827), Carlsbad (115,382), Santa Barbara (91,364), and Santa Fe Springs (population 17,630) **_all_ winning one-thousand dollars each after taxes!** And that is based on only 17.9% of the state's population contributing. That is over **$2.4 billion** paid out to Californians each year after taxes!

COLORADO – "The Centennial State"

Odds of Winning in Colorado 293 to 1

WEEKLY DRAWING BASED ON AVERAGE PURCHASE OF $10 (2 TICKETS)
Participants: 1,390,123 or 24.1% of the State Population
State Pool: $13,901,230
State & Local Combined Sales Tax (7.65%): $1,063,444
Federal ASP Tax (24%): $3,336,295
Citizens Prize Pool: $9,501,491
WEEKLY DRAWING RESULTS: 9,501 Prizes of $1000 + 1 Mini Prize of $491

1 YEAR PROJECTION: BASED ON AVERAGE PURCHASE OF 2 TICKETS ($10)
Colorado Annual Revenue: $722,863,960
Colorado Annual Tax Revenue: $55,299,088
Annual Federal Tax Revenue: $173,487,340
Annual Winning Tickets of $1000 in Colorado: **494,052**
CASH PAID YEARLY TO COLORADANS AFTER TAXES: $494,077,532

ROCKY MOUNTAIN HIGH!

Winning tickets awarded to the people of Colorado would be the equivalent of every man, woman, and child of Fort Collins (population 170,243), Pueblo (112,361), Boulder (105,673), Erie (27,003), Columbine (25,094), Steamboat Springs (13,214), Cherry Creek (12,601), Rifle (9,706), Craig (9,022), and Aspen (population 7,401) **_all_ winning one-thousand dollars each after taxes!** And this is based on only 24.1% of the state's population contributing. The American Stimulus Program can provide over **$500,000,000** to the economy of Colorado each year!

CONNECTICUT – "The Constitution State"

Odds of Winning in Connecticut 287 to 1

WEEKLY DRAWING BASED ON AVERAGE PURCHASE OF $10 (2 TICKETS)

Participants: 822,460 or 23% of the State Population
State Pool: $8,224,600
State & Local Combined Sales Tax (6.35%): $522,262
Federal ASP Tax (24%): $1,973,904
Citizens Prize Pool: $5,728,434
WEEKLY DRAWING RESULTS: 5,728 Prizes of $1000 + 1 Mini Prize of $434

1 YEAR PROJECTION: BASED ON AVERAGE PURCHASE OF 2 TICKETS ($10)

Connecticut Annual Revenue: $427,679,200
Connecticut Annual Tax Revenue: $27,157,624
Annual Federal Tax Revenue: $102,643,008
Annual Winning Tickets of $1000 in Connecticut: **297,856**
CASH PAID YEARLY TO CONNECTICUTERS AFTER TAXES: $297,878,568

NUTMEGGER CASH!

Winning tickets awarded to the people of Connecticut would be the equivalent of every man, woman, and child of New Haven (population 130,850), Manchester (28,899), East Haven (28,860), Westport (27,840), New London (26,919), Ansonia (18,607), Orange (13,937), Greenwich (13,303), and Riverside (population 8,414) **_all_ winning one-thousand dollars each after taxes!** And this is based on only 23% of the state's population contributing. The American Stimulus Program can add over **$300,000,000** to the economy of Connecticut each year!

DELAWARE – "The First State"

Odds of Winning in Delaware 263 to 1

WEEKLY DRAWING BASED ON AVERAGE PURCHASE OF $10 (2 TICKETS)

Participants: 221,907 or 22.8% of the State Population
State Pool: $2,219,070
State & Local Combined Sales Tax (0%): $0
Federal ASP Tax (24%): $532,576
Citizens Prize Pool: $1,686,494
WEEKLY DRAWING RESULTS: 1,686 Prizes of $1000 + 1 Mini Prize of $494

1 YEAR PROJECTION: BASED ON AVERAGE PURCHASE OF 2 TICKETS ($10)

Delaware Annual Revenue: $115,391,640
Delaware Annual Tax Revenue: $0
Annual Federal Tax Revenue: $27,693,952
Annual Winning Tickets of $1000 in Delaware: **87,672**
CASH PAID YEARLY TO DELAWAREANS AFTER TAXES: $87,697,688

THE LAND OF THRASHER'S, SCRAPPLE, AND THE KITCHEN SINK!

Winning tickets awarded to the people of Delaware would be the equivalent of every man, woman, and child of Newark (population 33,515), Pine Creek Valley (10,664), Wilmington Manor (7,902), Georgetown (7,563), Edgemoor (6,471), Newcastle (5,392), Laurel (4,356), Highland Acres (3,645), Milton (3,012), Riverview (2,684), and Ocean View (population 2,190) *__all__* **winning one-thousand dollars each after taxes!** And this is with only 22.8% of the state's population contributing. The American Stimulus Program can add over **$87,000,000** to the economy of Delaware each year!

FLORIDA – "The Sunshine State"

Odds of Winning in Florida 290 to 1

<u>WEEKLY DRAWING BASED ON AVERAGE PURCHASE OF $10 (2 TICKETS)</u>

Participants: 4,710,019 or 21.9% of the State Population
State Pool: $47,100,190
State & Local Combined Sales Tax (7.05%): $3,320,563
Federal ASP Tax (24%): $11,304,045
Citizens Prize Pool: $32,475,582
WEEKLY DRAWING RESULTS: 32,475 Prizes of $1000 + 1 Mini Prize of $582

<u>1 YEAR PROJECTION: BASED ON AVERAGE PURCHASE OF 2 TICKETS ($10)</u>

Florida Annual Revenue: $2,449,209,880
Florida Annual Tax Revenue: $172,669,276
Annual Federal Tax Revenue: $587,810,340
Annual Winning Tickets of $1000 in Florida: **1,688,700**
CASH PAID YEARLY TO FLORIDIANS AFTER TAXES: $1,688,730,264

<u>SERIOUS MONEY!</u>

Winning tickets awarded to the people of Florida would be the equivalent of every man, woman, and child of Miami (population 467,963), Orlando (287,442), Tallahassee (194,500), Fort Lauderdale (182,437), Gainesville (133,997), Boca Raton (99,805), Miami Beach (88,885), Largo (84,948), Boynton Beach (78,679), and Daytona Beach (population 69,186) **_all_ winning one-thousand dollars each after taxes!** And this is with only 21.9% of the state's population contributing. That is over **$1.6 BILLION** paid out to Floridians each year after taxes! **1,600,000,000!**

GEORGIA – "The Peach State"

Odds of Winning in Georgia 291 to 1

WEEKLY DRAWING BASED ON AVERAGE PURCHASE OF $10 (2 TICKETS)

Participants: 2,057,366 or 19.3% of the State Population
State Pool: $20,573,660
State & Local Combined Sales Tax (7.31%): $1,503,934
Federal ASP Tax (24%): $4,937,678
Citizens Prize Pool: $14,132,048
WEEKLY DRAWING RESULTS: 14,132 Prizes of $1000 + 1 Mini Prize of $48

1 YEAR PROJECTION: BASED ON AVERAGE PURCHASE OF 2 TICKETS ($10)

Georgia Annual Revenue: $1,069,830,320
Georgia Annual Tax Revenue: $78,204,568
Annual Federal Tax Revenue: $256,759,256
Annual Winning Tickets of $1000 in Georgia: **734,864**
CASH PAID YEARLY TO GEORGIANS AFTER TAXES: $734,866,496

THANK YOU KINDLY!

Winning tickets awarded to the people of Georgia would be the equivalent of every man, woman, and child of Columbus (population 195,769), Savannah (144,464), Sandy Springs (109,452), Albany (72,130), Marietta (60,867), Gainesville (43,232), Rome (36,716), Kennesaw (34,077), Union City (22,399), and Powder Springs (population 15,758) **_all_ winning one-thousand dollars each after taxes!** And this is based on only 19.3% of the state's population contributing. The American Stimulus Program can inject over **$750 MILLION** into the economy of Georgia each year!

HAWAII – "The Aloha State"

Odds of Winning in Hawaii 279 to 1

WEEKLY DRAWING BASED ON AVERAGE PURCHASE OF $10 (2 TICKETS)

Participants: 214,468 or 15.1% of the State Population
State Pool: $2,144,680
State & Local Combined Sales Tax (4.44%): $95,223
Federal ASP Tax (24%): $514,723
Citizens Prize Pool: $1,534,734
WEEKLY DRAWING RESULTS: 1,534 Prizes of $1000 + 1 Mini Prize of $734

1 YEAR PROJECTION: BASED ON AVERAGE PURCHASE OF 2 TICKETS ($10)

Hawaii Annual Revenue: $111,523,360
Hawaii Annual Tax Revenue: $4,951,596
Annual Federal Tax Revenue: $26,765,596
Annual Winning Tickets of $1000 in Hawaii: **79,768**
CASH PAID YEARLY TO HAWAIIANS AFTER TAXES: $79,806,168

MAHALO NUI LOA!

Winning tickets awarded to the people of Hawaii would be the equivalent of every man, woman, and child of Kihei (population 21,879), Ewa Beach (14,717), Makaha (8,740), Kula (7,541), Laie (6,111), Kalaheo (5,224), Kahaluu (4,339), Cain Cook (3,987), Volcano (3,269) and Hawaiian Acres (population 2,981) **_all_ winning one-thousand dollars each after taxes!** And this is based on only 15.1% of the state's population contributing. The American Stimulus Program can add over **$80,000,000** to the economy of Hawaii each year!

IDAHO – "The Gem State"

Odds of Winning in Idaho 286 to 1

WEEKLY DRAWING BASED ON AVERAGE PURCHASE OF $10 (2 TICKETS)

Participants: 345,127 or 19.3 % of the State Population
State Pool: $3,451,270
State & Local Combined Sales Tax (6.03%): $208,111
Federal ASP Tax (24%): $828,304
Citizens Prize Pool: $2,414,855
WEEKLY DRAWING RESULTS: 2,414 Prizes of $1000 + 1 Mini Prize of $855

1 YEAR PROJECTION: BASED ON AVERAGE PURCHASE OF 2 TICKETS ($10)

Idaho Annual Revenue: $179,466,040
Idaho Annual Tax Revenue: $10,821,772
Annual Federal Tax Revenue: $43,071,808
Annual Winning Tickets of $1000 in Idaho: **125,528**
CASH PAID YEARLY TO IDAHOANS AFTER TAXES: $125,572,460

POTATO CASH!

Winning tickets awarded to the people of Idaho would be the equivalent of every man, woman, and child of Post Falls (population 36,250), Moscow (25,702), Kuna (22,257), Star (10,532), Middleton (8,466), Emmett (7,054), Preston (5,557), Kimberly (4,054), Soda Springs (3,023), and Montpelier (population 2,538) **_all_ winning one-thousand dollars each after taxes!** And this is based on only 19.3% of the state's population contributing. The American Stimulus Program will bring over **$135,000,000** to the economy of Idaho each year!

ILLINOIS – "The Prairie State"

Odds of Winning in Illinois 299 to 1

WEEKLY DRAWING BASED ON AVERAGE PURCHASE OF $10 (2 TICKETS)

Participants: 2,768,212 or 21.8% of the State Population
State Pool: $27,682,120
State & Local Combined Sales Tax (9.08%): $2,513,536
Federal ASP Tax (24%): $6,643,708
Citizens Prize Pool: $18,524,876
WEEKLY DRAWING RESULTS: 18,524 Prizes of $1000 + 1 Mini Prize of $876

1 YEAR PROJECTION: BASED ON AVERAGE PURCHASE OF 2 TICKETS ($10)

Illinois Annual Revenue: $1,439,470,240
Illinois Annual Tax Revenue: $130,703,872
Annual Federal Tax Revenue: $345,472,816
Annual Winning Tickets of $1000 in Illinois: **963,248**
CASH PAID YEARLY TO ILLINOISANS AFTER TAXES: $963,293,552

PUT JIMMIES ON TOP!

Winning tickets awarded to the people of Illinois would be the equivalent of every man, woman, and child of Aurora (population 198,870), Joliet (148,227), Springfield (112,990), Peoria (108,194), Champaign (89,149), Cicero (79,943), Evanston (72,836), Mount Prospect (53,218), Oak Park (52,443), and Lombard (population 44,199) **_all_ winning one-thousand dollars each after taxes!** And this is based on only 21.8% of the state's population contributing. The American Stimulus Program could add over **$1 BILLION** to the economy of Illinois each year!

INDIANA – "The Hoosier State"

Odds of Winning in Indiana 290 to 1

WEEKLY DRAWING BASED ON AVERAGE PURCHASE OF $10 (2 TICKETS)

Participants: 1,367,479 or 20.3% of the State Population
State Pool: $13,674,790
State & Local Combined Sales Tax (7%): $957,235
Federal ASP Tax (24%): $3,281,949
Citizens Prize Pool: $9,435,606
WEEKLY DRAWING RESULTS: 9,435 Prizes of $1000 + 1 Mini Prize of $606

1 YEAR PROJECTION: BASED ON AVERAGE PURCHASE OF 2 TICKETS ($10)

Indiana Annual Revenue: $711,089,080
Indiana Annual Tax Revenue: $49,776,220
Annual Federal Tax Revenue: $170,661,348
Annual Winning Tickets of $1000 in Indiana: **490,620**
CASH PAID YEARLY TO THE CITIZENS OF INDIANA AFTER TAXES: $490,651,512

IT IS GONNA BE KNEE-HIGH BY THE FOURTH OF JULY!

Winning tickets awarded to the people of Indiana would be the equivalent of every man, woman, and child of Evansville (population 116,709), South Bend (102,028), Kokomo (58,175), Mishawaka (50,339), Plainfield (37,484), Goshen (33,722), Zionsville (28,343), Shelbyville (19,466), Jasper (15,714), Auburn (13,689), and Cedar Lake (population 13,223) _**all**_ **winning one-thousand dollars each after taxes!** And this is with only 20.3% of the state's population contributing. The American Stimulus Program can add over **$500,000,000** to the economy of Indiana each year!

IOWA – "The Hawkeye State"

Odds of Winning in Iowa 290 to 1

<u>WEEKLY DRAWING BASED ON AVERAGE PURCHASE OF $10 (2 TICKETS)</u>

Participants: 783,015 or 24.8% of the State Population
State Pool: $7,830,150
State & Local Combined Sales Tax (6.94%): $543,412
Federal ASP Tax (24%): $1,879,236
Citizens Prize Pool: $5,407,502
WEEKLY DRAWING RESULTS: 5,407 Prizes of $1000 + 1 Mini Prize of $502

<u>1 YEAR PROJECTION: BASED ON AVERAGE PURCHASE OF 2 TICKETS ($10)</u>

Iowa Annual Revenue: $407,167,800
Iowa Annual Tax Revenue: $28,257,424
Annual Federal Tax Revenue: $97,720,272
Annual Winning Tickets of $1000 in Iowa: **281,164**
CASH PAID YEARLY TO IOWANS AFTER TAXES: $281,190,104

<u>PORK QUEEN CAPITAL!</u>

Winning tickets awarded to the people of Iowa would be the equivalent of every man, woman, and child of Sioux City (population 81,382), Iowa City (78,440), Ames (67,962), Denison (8,406), Knoxville (7,144), Independence (6,165), Sergeant Bluff (5,085), Forest City (4,083), Williamsburg (3,131), and Atkins (population 2,007) **_all_ winning one-thousand dollars each after taxes!** And this is based on only 24.8% of the state's population contributing. The American Stimulus Program can add over **$300,000,000** to the economy of Iowa each year!

KANSAS – "The Sunflower State"

Odds of Winning in Kansas 297 to 1

<u>WEEKLY DRAWING BASED ON AVERAGE PURCHASE OF $10 (2 TICKETS)</u>
Participants: 592,201 or 20.3% of the State Population
State Pool: $5,922,010
State & Local Combined Sales Tax (8.68%): $514,030
Federal ASP Tax (24%): $1,421,282
Citizens Prize Pool: $3,986,698
WEEKLY DRAWING RESULTS: 3,986 Prizes of $1000 + 1 Mini Prize of $698

<u>1 YEAR PROJECTION: BASED ON AVERAGE PURCHASE OF 2 TICKETS ($10)</u>
Kansas Annual Revenue: $307,944,520
Kansas Annual Tax Revenue: $26,729,560
Annual Federal Tax Revenue: $73,906,664
Annual Winning Tickets of $1000 in Kansas: **207,272**
CASH PAID YEARLY TO KANSANS AFTER TAXES: $207,308,296

<u>MONEY SHOWER!</u>
  Winning tickets awarded to the people of Kansas would be the equivalent of every man, woman, and child of Topeka (population 125,092), Manhattan (54,749), Hayes (20,616), Great Bend (14,610), Augusta (9,360), Independence (8,348), Fort Scott (7,789), Eudora (6,166), and Colby (population 5,305) **<u>*all*</u> winning one-thousand dollars each after taxes!** And this is with only 20.3% of the state's population contributing. The American Stimulus Program can add over **$200,000,000** to the economy of Kansas each year!

KENTUCKY – "The Bluegrass State"

Odds of Winning in Kentucky 286 to 1

<u>**WEEKLY DRAWING BASED ON AVERAGE PURCHASE OF $10 (2 TICKETS)**</u>

Participants: 962,074 or 21.5% of the State Population
State Pool: $9,620,740
State & Local Combined Sales Tax (6%): $577,244
Federal ASP Tax (24%): $2,308,977
Citizens Prize Pool: $6,734,519
WEEKLY DRAWING RESULTS: 6,734 Prizes of $1000 + 1 Mini Prize of $519

<u>**1 YEAR PROJECTION: BASED ON AVERAGE PURCHASE OF 2 TICKETS ($10)**</u>

Kentucky Annual Revenue: $500,278,480
Kentucky Annual Tax Revenue: $30,016,688
Annual Federal Tax Revenue: $120,066,804
Annual Winning Tickets of $1000 in Kentucky: **350,168**
CASH PAID YEARLY TO KENTUCKIANS AFTER TAXES: $350,194,988

<u>**PRAISE THE LORD & PASS THE GRAVY!**</u>

Winning tickets awarded to the people of Kentucky would be the equivalent of every man, woman, and child of Bowling Green (population 71,623), Owensboro (60,323), Covington (40,136), Richmond (37,652), Georgetown (36,081), Elizabethtown (30,837), Paducah (24,672), Radcliff (23,218), Mount Washington (15,073), and Paris (population 9,846) <u>***all***</u> **winning one-thousand dollars each after taxes!** And this is based on only 21.5% of the state's population contributing. The American Stimulus Program can add over **$350,000,000** to the economy of Kentucky each year!

LOUISIANA – "The Pelican State"

Odds of Winning in Louisiana 301 to 1

WEEKLY DRAWING BASED ON AVERAGE PURCHASE OF $10 (2 TICKETS)

Participants: 1,014,516 or 21.8% of the State Population
State Pool: $10,145,160
State & Local Combined Sales Tax (9.52%): $965,819
Federal ASP Tax (24%): $2,434,838
Citizens Prize Pool: $6,744,503
WEEKLY DRAWING RESULTS: 6,744 Prizes of $1000 + 1 Mini Prize of $503

1 YEAR PROJECTION: BASED ON AVERAGE PURCHASE OF 2 TICKETS ($10)

Louisiana Annual Revenue: $527,548,320
Louisiana Annual Tax Revenue: $50,222,588
Annual Federal Tax Revenue: $126,611,576
Annual Winning Tickets of $1000 in Louisiana: **350,688**
CASH PAID YEARLY TO LOUISIANIANS AFTER TAXES: $350,714,156

PASS A GOOD TIME!

Winning tickets awarded to the people of Louisiana would be the equivalent of every man, woman, and child of Baton Rouge (population 216,701), Monroe (46,737), Hammond (20,820), Bayou Blue (11,682), Raceland (10,686), Eunice (9,817), Old Jefferson (8,065), Oakdale (7,510), Walker (6,048), and Grambling (population 5,154) _**all**_ **winning one-thousand dollars each after taxes!** And this is based on only 21.8% of the state's population contributing. The American Stimulus Program can add well over **$350,000,000** to the economy of Louisiana each year!

MAINE – "The Pine Tree State"

Odds of Winning in Maine 284 to 1

WEEKLY DRAWING BASED ON AVERAGE PURCHASE OF $10 (2 TICKETS)

Participants: 373,918 or 27.8% of the State Population
State Pool: $3,739,180
State & Local Combined Sales Tax (5.50%): $205,654
Federal ASP Tax (24%): $897,403
Citizens Prize Pool: $2,636,123
WEEKLY DRAWING RESULTS: 2,636 Prizes of $1000 + 1 Mini Prize of $123

1 YEAR PROJECTION: BASED ON AVERAGE PURCHASE OF 2 TICKETS ($10)

Maine Annual Revenue: $194,437,360
Maine Annual Tax Revenue: $10,694,008
Annual Federal Tax Revenue: $46,664,956
Annual Winning Tickets of $1000 in Maine: **137,072**
CASH PAID YEARLY TO MAINERS AFTER TAXES: $137,078,396

AYUH!

Winning tickets awarded to the people of Maine would be the equivalent of every man, woman, and child of Bangor (population 32,167), Westbrook (19,760), Brunswick (15,244), Brewer (9,127), Bath (8,407), Rockland (7,102), Skowhegan (6,434), Lisbon Falls (4,189), Fairfield (3,152), and Randolph (population 1,982) **_all_ winning one-thousand dollars each after taxes!** And this is based on only 27.8% of the state's population contributing. The American Stimulus Program can pay out nearly **$140,000,000** each year to the people of Maine!

MARYLAND – "The Free State"

Odds of Winning in Maryland 286 to 1

WEEKLY DRAWING BASED ON AVERAGE PURCHASE OF $10 (2 TICKETS)

Participants: 1,390,723 or 23% of the State Population
State Pool: $13,907,230
State & Local Combined Sales Tax (6%): $834,433
Federal ASP Tax (24%): $3,337,735
Citizens Prize Pool: $9,735,062
WEEKLY DRAWING RESULTS: 9,735 Prizes of $1000 + 1 Mini Prize of $62

1 YEAR PROJECTION: BASED ON AVERAGE PURCHASE OF 2 TICKETS ($10)

Maryland Annual Revenue: $723,175,960
Maryland Annual Tax Revenue: $43,390,516
Annual Federal Tax Revenue: $173,562,220
Annual Winning Tickets of $1000 in Maryland: **506,220**
CASH PAID YEARLY TO MARYLANDERS AFTER TAXES: $506,233,224

HEY, HON!

Winning tickets awarded to the people of Maryland would be the equivalent of every man, woman, and child of Columbia (population 103,663), Germantown (90,844), Rockville (70,088), Bethesda (62,448), Wheaton (50,459), Clinton (40,027), Bel Air North (31,582), Fairland (24,831), Lake Shore (20,260), and Forestville (population 11,719) **_all_ winning one-thousand dollars each after taxes!** And this is based on only 23% of the state's population contributing. The American Stimulus Program can pay out over **$500,000,000** each year to the people of Maryland!

MASSACHUSETTS – "The Bay State"

Odds of Winning in Massachusetts 287 to 1

WEEKLY DRAWING BASED ON AVERAGE PURCHASE OF $10 (2 TICKETS)

Participants: 1,662,523 or 24.1% of the State Population
State Pool: $16,625,230
State & Local Combined Sales Tax (6.25%): $1,039,076
Federal ASP Tax (24%): $3,990,055
Citizens Prize Pool: $11,596,099
WEEKLY DRAWING RESULTS: 11,596 Prizes of $1000 + 1 Mini Prize of $99

1 YEAR PROJECTION: BASED ON AVERAGE PURCHASE OF 2 TICKETS ($10)

Massachusetts Annual Revenue: $864,511,960
Massachusetts Annual Tax Revenue: $54,031,952
Annual Federal Tax Revenue: $207,482,860
Annual Winning Tickets of $1000 in Massachusetts: **602,992**
CASH PAID YEARLY TO BAY STATERS AFTER TAXES: $602,997,148

WICKED!

Winning tickets awarded to the people of Massachusetts would be the equivalent of every man, woman, and child in Worcester (population 186,433), Springfield (155,472), Quincy (94,948), Lawrence (80,760), Malden (60,860), and Wilmington (population 23,658) **_all_ winning one-thousand dollars each after taxes!** And this is based on only 24.1% of the state's population contributing. The American Stimulus Program can pay out over **$600,000,000** each year to the people of Massachusetts!

MICHIGAN – "The Great Lakes State"

Odds of Winning in Michigan 286 to 1

WEEKLY DRAWING BASED ON AVERAGE PURCHASE OF $10 (2 TICKETS)

Participants: 2,399,642 or 24% of the State Population
State Pool: $23,996,420
State & Local Combined Sales Tax (6%): $1,439,785
Federal ASP Tax (24%): $5,759,140
Citizens Prize Pool: $16,797,495
WEEKLY DRAWING RESULTS: 16,797 Prizes of $1000 + 1 Mini Prize of $495

1 YEAR PROJECTION: BASED ON AVERAGE PURCHASE OF 2 TICKETS ($10)

Michigan Annual Revenue: $1,247,813,840
Michigan Annual Tax Revenue: $74,868,820
Annual Federal Tax Revenue: $299,475,280
Annual Winning Tickets of $1000 in Michigan: **873,444**
CASH PAID YEARLY TO THE CITIZENS OF MICHIGAN AFTER TAXES:
$873,469,740

CASH FOR MORE THAN JUST THE MITTEN!

Winning tickets awarded to the people of Michigan would be the equivalent of every man, woman, and child of Grand Rapids (population 205,289), Warren (134,370), Ann Arbor (123,062), Lansing (120,921), Flint (94,867), Kalamazoo (76,497), Pontiac (59,570), and Muskegon (population 36,903) **_all_ winning one-thousand dollars each after taxes!** And this is with only 24% of the state's population contributing. The American Stimulus Program can pay out over **$900,000,000** to the economy of Michigan each year!

MINNESOTA – "The North Star State"

Odds of Winning in Minnesota 292 to 1

WEEKLY DRAWING BASED ON AVERAGE PURCHASE OF $10 (2 TICKETS)

Participants: 1,472,406 or 26.1% of the State Population
State Pool: $14,724,060
State & Local Combined Sales Tax (7.46%): $1,098,414
Federal ASP Tax (24%): $3,533,774
Citizens Prize Pool: $10,091,872
WEEKLY DRAWING RESULTS: 10,091 Prizes of $1000 + 1 Mini Prize of $872

1 YEAR PROJECTION: BASED ON AVERAGE PURCHASE OF 2 TICKETS ($10)

Minnesota Annual Revenue: $765,651,120
Minnesota Annual Tax Revenue: $57,117,528
Annual Federal Tax Revenue: $183,756,248
Annual Winning Tickets of $1000 in Minnesota: **524,732**
CASH PAID YEARLY TO MINNESOTANS AFTER TAXES: $524,777,344

UFF-DA!

Winning tickets awarded to the people of Minnesota would be the equivalent of every man, woman, and child of St. Paul (population 311,895), Eagan (67,097), Minnetonka (54,861), Roseville (37,281), Chaska (27,687), and Owatonna (population 25,950) _**all**_ **winning one-thousand dollars each after taxes!** And this is based on only 26.1% of the state's population contributing. The American Stimulus Program can pay out over **$500,000,000** to the people of Minnesota each year!

MISSISSIPPI – "The Magnolia State"

Odds of Winning in Mississippi 290 to 1

WEEKLY DRAWING BASED ON AVERAGE PURCHASE OF $10 (2 TICKETS)

Participants: 604,678 or 20.3% of the State Population
State Pool: $6,046,780
State & Local Combined Sales Tax (7.07%): $427,507
Federal ASP Tax (24%): $1,451,227
Citizens Prize Pool: $4,168,046
WEEKLY DRAWING RESULTS: 4,168 Prizes of $1000 + 1 Mini Prize of $46

1 YEAR PROJECTION: BASED ON AVERAGE PURCHASE OF 2 TICKETS ($10)

Mississippi Annual Revenue: $314,432,560
Mississippi Annual Tax Revenue: $22,230,364
Annual Federal Tax Revenue: $75,463,804
Annual Winning Tickets of $1000 in Mississippi: **216,736**
CASH PAID YEARLY TO MISSISSIPPIANS AFTER TAXES: $216,738,392

MONEY FOR YOUR MAMA' N EM!

Winning tickets awarded to the people of Mississippi would be the equivalent of every man, woman, and child of Gulfport (population 72,670), Tupelo (38,030), Madison (25,718), Columbus (23,375), Natchez (14,809), Clarksdale (14,300), Brookhaven (11,997), and Yazoo City (population 10,607) _**all**_ **winning one-thousand dollars each after taxes!** And this is with only 20.3% of the state's population contributing! That is over **$200,000,000** paid directly to the citizens of Mississippi each year!

MISSOURI – "The Show-Me State"

Odds of Winning in Missouri 295 to 1

WEEKLY DRAWING BASED ON AVERAGE PURCHASE OF $10 (2 TICKETS)

Participants: 1,404,302 or 22.8% of the State Population
State Pool: $14,043,020
State & Local Combined Sales Tax (8.18%): $1,148,719
Federal ASP Tax (24%): $3,370,324
Citizens Prize Pool: $9,523,977
WEEKLY DRAWING RESULTS: 9,523 Prizes of $1000 + 1 Mini Prize of $977

1 YEAR PROJECTION: BASED ON AVERAGE PURCHASE OF 2 TICKETS ($10)

Missouri Annual Revenue: $730,237,040
Missouri Annual Tax Revenue: $59,733,388
Annual Federal Tax Revenue: $175,256,848
Annual Winning Tickets of $1000 in Missouri: **495,196**
CASH PAID YEARLY TO MISSOURIANS AFTER TAXES: $495,246,804

SHOW ME THE MONEY!

Winning tickets awarded to the people of Missouri would be the equivalent of every man, woman, and child in St. Louis (population 293,792), O'Fallon (90,684), Jefferson City (42,588), Liberty (33,501), Ozark (21,338), and Troy (population 13,006) **_all_ winning one-thousand dollars each after taxes!** And this is based on only 22.8% of the state's population contributing! The American Stimulus Program can inject over **$500,000,000** into the state of Missouri each year!

MONTANA – "The Treasure State"

Odds of Winning in Montana 263 to 1

WEEKLY DRAWING BASED ON AVERAGE PURCHASE OF $10 (2 TICKETS)

Participants: 248,573 or 23.3% of the State Population
State Pool: $2,485,730
State & Local Combined Sales Tax (0%): 0
Federal ASP Tax (24%): $596,575
Citizens Prize Pool: $1,889,155
WEEKLY DRAWING RESULTS: 1,889 Prizes of $1000 + 1 Mini Prize of $155

1 YEAR PROJECTION: BASED ON AVERAGE PURCHASE OF 2 TICKETS ($10)

Montana Annual Revenue: $129,257,960
Montana Tax Revenue: $0
Annual Federal Tax Revenue: $31,021,900
Annual Winning Tickets of $1000 in Montana: **98,228**
CASH PAID YEARLY TO MONTANANS AFTER TAXES: $98,236,060

FINER THAN FROG HAIR!

Winning tickets awarded to the people of Montana would be the equivalent of every man, woman, and child of Butte (population 34,676), Helena (33,525), Miles City (8,237), Bigfork (4,626), Glendive (4,618), Lolo (3,780), Big Sky (3,098), and Montana City (population 2,796) **_all_ winning one-thousand dollars each after taxes!** And this is with only 23.3% of the state's population contributing! The Citizen Stimulus Drawing can help to add over **$100,000,000** into the economy of Montana each year!

NEBRASKA – "The Cornhusker State"

Odds of Winning in Nebraska 290 to 1

WEEKLY DRAWING BASED ON AVERAGE PURCHASE OF $10 (2 TICKETS)

Participants: 422,104 or 21.8% of the State Population
State Pool: $4,221,040
State & Local Combined Sales Tax (6.93%): $292,518
Federal ASP Tax (24%): $1,013,049
Citizens Prize Pool: $2,915,473
WEEKLY DRAWING RESULTS: 2,915 Prizes of $1000 + 1 Mini Prize of $473

1 YEAR PROJECTION: BASED ON AVERAGE PURCHASE OF 2 TICKETS ($10)

Nebraska Annual Revenue: $219,494,080
Nebraska Annual Tax Revenue: $15,210,936
Annual Federal Tax Revenue: $52,678,548
Annual Winning Tickets of $1000 in Nebraska: **151,580**
CASH PAID YEARLY TO NEBRASKANS AFTER TAXES: $151,604,596

MONEY GREASES THE AXLE!

Winning tickets awarded to the people of Nebraska would be the equivalent of every man, woman, and child of Grand Island (population 51,440), Norfolk (26,731), Hastings (24,972), Scottsbluff (14,621), Gering (8,101), Nebraska City (7,265), Aurora (4,581), Broken Bow (3,582), and Kimball (population 2,260) **_all_ winning one-thousand dollars each after taxes!** And this with only 21.8% of the state's population contributing! The Citizen Stimulus Drawing can help to add over **$150,000,000** to the economy of Nebraska each year!

NEVADA – "The Silver State"

Odds of Winning in Nevada 296 to 1

WEEKLY DRAWING BASED ON AVERAGE PURCHASE OF $10 (2 TICKETS)

Participants: 562,692 or 18.2% of the State Population
State Pool: $5,626,920
State & Local Combined Sales Tax (8.32%): $468,159
Federal ASP Tax (24%): $1,350,460
Citizens Prize Pool: $3,808,301
WEEKLY DRAWING RESULTS: 3,808 Prizes of $1000 + 1 Mini Prize of $301

1 YEAR PROJECTION: BASED ON AVERAGE PURCHASE OF 2 TICKETS ($10)

Nevada Annual Revenue: $292,599,840
Nevada Annual Tax Revenue: $24,344,268
Annual Federal Tax Revenue: $70,223,920
Annual Winning Tickets of $1000 in Nevada: **198,016**
CASH PAID YEARLY TO NEVADANS AFTER TAXES: $198,031,652

NE-VA-DA!

Winning tickets awarded to the people of Nevada would be the equivalent of every man, woman, and child of Carson City (population 56,336), Pahrump (36,174), Sun Valley (20,683), Elko (20,467), Mesquite (20,131), Boulder City (16,153), Winnemucca (7,675), Laughlin (7,502), and Moapa Valley (population 6,843) _**all winning one-thousand dollars each after taxes!**_ And this is with only 18.2% of the state's population contributing! The American Stimulus Program can help to add over **$200,000,000** to the economy of Nevada each year!

NEW HAMPSHIRE – "The Granite State"

Odds of Winning in New Hampshire 263 to 1

WEEKLY DRAWING BASED ON AVERAGE PURCHASE OF $10 (2 TICKETS)

Participants: 372,148 or 27.3% of the State Population
State Pool: $3,721,480
State & Local Combined Sales Tax (0%): $0
Federal ASP Tax (24%): $893,155
Citizens Prize Pool: $2,828,325
WEEKLY DRAWING RESULTS: 2,828 Prizes of $1000 + 1 Mini Prize of $325

1 YEAR PROJECTION: BASED ON AVERAGE PURCHASE OF 2 TICKETS ($10)

New Hampshire Annual Revenue: $193,516,960
New Hampshire Annual Tax Revenue: $0
Annual Federal Tax Revenue: $46,444,060
Annual Winning Tickets of $1000 in New Hampshire: **147,056**
CASH PAID YEARLY TO NEW HAMPSHIRITES AFTER TAXES: $147,072,900

WICKED GOOD!

Winning tickets awarded to the people of New Hampshire would be the equivalent of every man, woman, and child of Concord (population 43,840), Dover (32,343), Rochester (32,224), Durham (11,101), Hampton (9,235), Hanover (8,591), and Hudson (population 7,591) *all* **winning one-thousand dollars each after taxes!** And this with only 27.3% of the state's population contributing! The American Stimulus Program can help add nearly $150,000,000 to New Hampshire's economy each year!

NEW JERSEY – "The Garden State"

Odds of Winning in New Jersey 288 to 1

WEEKLY DRAWING BASED ON AVERAGE PURCHASE OF $10 (2 TICKETS)

Participants: 1,937,023 or 21.8% of the State Population
State Pool: $19,370,230
State & Local Combined Sales Tax (6.60%): $1,278,435
Federal ASP Tax (24%): $4,648,855
Citizens Prize Pool: $13,442,940
WEEKLY DRAWING RESULTS: 13,442 Prizes of $1000 + 1 Mini Prize of $940

1 YEAR PROJECTION: BASED ON AVERAGE PURCHASE OF 2 TICKETS ($10)

New Jersey Annual Revenue: $1,007,251,960
New Jersey Annual Tax Revenue: $66,478,620
Annual Federal Tax Revenue: $241,740,460
Annual Winning Tickets of $1000 in New Jersey: **698,984**
CASH PAID YEARLY TO NEW JERSEYITES AFTER TAXES: $699,032,880

DOWN THE SHORE & BEYOND!

Winning tickets awarded to the people of New Jersey would be the equivalent of every man, woman, and child of Newark (population 282,862), Toms River (88,712), Trenton (84,386), Camden (73,811), New Brunswick (55,960), Hoboken (53,445), Atlantic City (37,054), and Morristown (population 18,997) _**all**_ **winning one-thousand dollars each after taxes!** And this is with only 21.8% of the state's population contributing! The American Stimulus Program can add over **$750,000,000** to the economy of New Jersey each year!

NEW MEXICO – "The Land of Enchantment"

Odds of Winning in New Mexico 293 to 1

WEEKLY DRAWING BASED ON AVERAGE PURCHASE OF $10 (2 TICKETS)

Participants: 399,159 or 19% of the State Population
State Pool: $3,991,590
State & Local Combined Sales Tax (7.82%): $312,142
Federal ASP Tax (24%): $957,981
Citizens Prize Pool: $2,721,467
WEEKLY DRAWING RESULTS: 2,721 Prizes of $1000 + 1 Mini Prize of $467

1 YEAR PROJECTION: BASED ON AVERAGE PURCHASE OF 2 TICKETS ($10)

New Mexico Annual Revenue: $207,562,680
New Mexico Annual Tax Revenue: $16,231,384
Annual Federal Tax Revenue: $49,815,012
Annual Winning Tickets of $1000 in New Mexico: **141,492**
CASH PAID YEARLY TO NEW MEXICANS AFTER TAXES: $141,516,284

RED AND LOTS OF GREEN!

Winning tickets awarded to the people of New Mexico would be the equivalent of every man, woman, and child of Roswell (population 46,977), Hobbs (37,465), Carlsbad (29,383), Los Alamos (12,373), Silver City (9,283), and Aztec (population 6,322) **_all_ winning one-thousand dollars each after taxes!** And this is with only 19% of the state's population contributing! The American Stimulus Program can add over **$150,000,000** to the economy of New Mexico each year!

NEW YORK – "The Empire State"

Odds of Winning in New York 296 to 1

WEEKLY DRAWING BASED ON AVERAGE PURCHASE OF $10 (2 TICKETS)

Participants: 3,860,726 or 19.8% of the State Population
State Pool: $38,607,260
State & Local Combined Sales Tax (8.52%): $3,289,338
Federal ASP Tax (24%): $9,265,742
Citizens Prize Pool: $26,052,180
WEEKLY DRAWING RESULTS: 26,052 Prizes of $1000 + 1 Mini Prize of $180

1 YEAR PROJECTION: BASED ON AVERAGE PURCHASE OF 2 TICKETS ($10)

New York Annual Revenue: $2,007,577,520
New York Annual Tax Revenue: $171,045,576
Annual Federal Tax Revenue: $481,818,584
Annual Winning Tickets of $1000 in New York: **1,354,704**
CASH PAID YEARLY TO NEW YORKERS AFTER TAXES: $1,354,713,360

ONLY IN NEW YORK!

Winning tickets awarded to the people of New York would be the equivalent of every man, woman, and child of Buffalo (population 255,244), Rochester (203,792), Yonkers (199,021), Syracuse (140,987), Albany (96,853), New Rochelle (77,912), Mount Vernon (66,955), Schenectady (66,107), White Plains (58,823), Niagara Falls (47,606), Binghamton (43,843), Brighton (36,447), and Ithaca (population 31,755) **_all_ winning one-thousand dollars each after taxes!** And this is with only 19.8% of the state's population contributing! The American Stimulus Program can add over **$1.5 BILLION** to the economy of New York each year! Unbelievable!

NORTH CAROLINA – "The Tar Heel State"

Odds of Winning in North Carolina 290 to 1

WEEKLY DRAWING BASED ON AVERAGE PURCHASE OF $10 (2 TICKETS)

Participants: 2,370,782 or 22.6% of the State Population
State Pool: $23,707,820
State & Local Combined Sales Tax (6.97%): $1,652,435
Federal ASP Tax (24%): $5,689,876
Citizens Prize Pool: $16,365,509
WEEKLY DRAWING RESULTS: 16,365 Prizes of $1000 + 1 Mini Prize of $509

1 YEAR PROJECTION: BASED ON AVERAGE PURCHASE OF 2 TICKETS ($10)

North Carolina Annual Revenue: $1,232,806,640
North Carolina Annual Tax Revenue: $85,926,620
Annual Federal Tax Revenue: $295,873,552
Annual Winning Tickets of $1000 in North Carolina: **850,980**
CASH PAID YEARLY TO NORTH CAROLINIANS AFTER TAXES: $851,006,468

BLUE DREAMS!

Winning tickets awarded to the people of North Carolina would be the equivalent of every man, woman, and child of Greensboro (population 299,946), Winston-Salem (251,762), Concord (98,842), Chapel Hill (59,606), Wake Forest (48,048), Monroe (36,183), Goldsboro (32,252), and Kinston (population 19,643) **_all_ winning one-thousand dollars each after taxes!** And this is based on only 22.6% of the state's population contributing! The American Stimulus Program can add over **$900,000,000** to the economy of North Carolina each year!

NORTH DAKOTA – "The Peace Garden State"

Odds of Winning in North Dakota 289 to 1

WEEKLY DRAWING BASED ON AVERAGE PURCHASE OF $10 (2 TICKETS)

Participants: 172,180 or 22.6% of the State Population
State Pool: $1,721,800
State & Local Combined Sales Tax (6.86%): $118,115
Federal ASP Tax (24%): $413,232
Citizens Prize Pool: $1,190,453
WEEKLY DRAWING RESULTS: 1,190 Prizes of $1000 + 1 Mini Prize of $453

1 YEAR PROJECTION: BASED ON AVERAGE PURCHASE OF 2 TICKETS ($10)

North Dakota Annual Revenue: $89,533,600
North Dakota Annual Tax Revenue: $6,141,980
Annual Federal Tax Revenue: $21,488,064
Annual Winning Tickets of $1000 in North Dakota: **61,880**
CASH PAID YEARLY TO NORTH DAKOTANS AFTER TAXES: $61,903,556

OH, FER CUTE!

Winning tickets awarded to the people of North Dakota would be the equivalent of every man, woman, and child of Williston (population 25,810), Dickinson (21,835), Watford City (7,348), Grafton (4,157), and Belcourt (population 2,038), **_all_ winning one-thousand dollars each after taxes!** And this is with only 22.6% of the state's population contributing! The American Stimulus Program can add nearly **$70,000,000** to the economy of North Dakota each year!

OHIO – "The Buckeye State"

Odds of Winning in Ohio 291 to 1

WEEKLY DRAWING BASED ON AVERAGE PURCHASE OF $10 (2 TICKETS)

Participants: 2,748,243 or 23.5% of the State Population
State Pool: $27,482,430
State & Local Combined Sales Tax (7.17%): $1,970,490
Federal ASP Tax (24%): $6,595,783
Citizens Prize Pool: $18,916,157
WEEKLY DRAWING RESULTS: 18,916 Prizes of $1000 + 1 Mini Prize of $157

1 YEAR PROJECTION: BASED ON AVERAGE PURCHASE OF 2 TICKETS ($10)

Ohio Annual Revenue: $1,429,086,360
Ohio Annual Tax Revenue: $102,465,480
Annual Federal Tax Revenue: $342,980,716
Annual Winning Tickets of $1000 in Ohio: **983,632**
CASH PAID YEARLY TO OHIOANS AFTER TAXES: $983,640,164

O-H-I-O!

Winning tickets awarded to the people of Ohio would be the equivalent of every man, woman, and child of Cleveland (population 379,233), Cincinnati (306,487), Dayton (139,756), Youngstown (65,422), Delaware (40,926), Kent (29,448), and Painesville (population 19,959) *all* **winning one-thousand dollars each after taxes!** And this with only 23.5% of the state's population contributing! The American Stimulus Program can add over **$1 BILLION** to the economy of Ohio each year!

OKLAHOMA – "The Sooner State"

Odds of Winning in Oklahoma 298 to 1

WEEKLY DRAWING BASED ON AVERAGE PURCHASE OF $10 (2 TICKETS)

Participants: 726,496 or 18.4% of the State Population
State Pool: $7,264,960
State & Local Combined Sales Tax (8.94%): $649,487
Federal ASP Tax (24%): $1,743,590
Citizens Prize Pool: $4,871,883
WEEKLY DRAWING RESULTS: 4,871 Prizes of $1000 + 1 Mini Prize of $883

1 YEAR PROJECTION: BASED ON AVERAGE PURCHASE OF 2 TICKETS ($10)

Oklahoma Annual Revenue: $377,777,920
Oklahoma Annual Tax Revenue: $33,773,324
Annual Federal Tax Revenue: $90,666,680
Annual Winning Tickets of $1000 in Oklahoma: **253,292**
CASH PAID YEARLY TO OKLAHOMANS AFTER TAXES: $253,337,916

OKIE CASH!

Winning tickets awarded to the people of Oklahoma would be the equivalent of every man, woman, and child of Norman (population 126,377), Moore (63,117), Shawnee (31,606), Sand Springs (19,765), and Miami (population 12,880), **_all_ winning one-thousand dollars each after taxes!** And this is with only 18.4% of the state's population contributing! The American Stimulus Program can add over **$250,000,000** to the economy of Oklahoma each year!

OREGON – "The Beaver State"

Odds of Winning in Oregon 263 to 1

WEEKLY DRAWING BASED ON AVERAGE PURCHASE OF $10 (2 TICKETS)

Participants: 1,000,688 or 23.7% of the State Population

State Pool: $10,006,880

State & Local Combined Sales Tax (0%): $0

Federal ASP Tax (24%): $2,401,651

Citizens Prize Pool: $7,605,229

WEEKLY DRAWING RESULTS: 7,605 Prizes of $1000 + 1 Mini Prize of $229

1 YEAR PROJECTION: BASED ON AVERAGE PURCHASE OF 2 TICKETS ($10)

Oregon Annual Revenue: $520,357,760

Oregon Annual Tax Revenue: $0

Annual Federal Tax Revenue: $124,885,852

Annual Winning Tickets of $1000 in Oregon: **395,460**

CASH PAID YEARLY TO OREGONIANS AFTER TAXES: $395,471,908

SOME CASH WITH YOUR WINE!

Winning tickets awarded to the people of Oregon would be the equivalent of every man, woman, and child of Eugene (population 178,829), Bend (105,418), Springfield (64,717), Keizer (40,704), and Veneta (population 5,290) _**all**_ **winning one-thousand dollars each after taxes!** And this is with only 23.7% of the state's population contributing! The American Stimulus Program can add over **$400,000,000** to the economy of Oregon each year!

PENNSYLVANIA – "The Keystone State"

Odds of Winning in Pennsylvania 287 to 1

WEEKLY DRAWING BASED ON AVERAGE PURCHASE OF $10 (2 TICKETS)

Participants: 3,082,739 or 24.1% of the State Population
State Pool: $30,827,390
State & Local Combined Sales Tax (6.34%): $1,945,456
Federal ASP Tax (24%): $7,398,573
Citizens Prize Pool: $21,483,361
WEEKLY DRAWING RESULTS: 21,483 Prizes of $1000 + 1 Mini Prize of $361

1 YEAR PROJECTION: BASED ON AVERAGE PURCHASE OF 2 TICKETS ($10)

Pennsylvania Annual Revenue: $1,603,024,280
Pennsylvania Annual Tax Revenue: $101,631,712
Annual Federal Tax Revenue: $384,725,796
Annual Winning Tickets of $1000 in Pennsylvania: **1,117,116**
CASH PAID YEARLY TO PENNSYLVANIANS AFTER TAXES: $1,117,134,772

LIBERTY!

Winning tickets awarded to the people of Pennsylvania would be the equivalent of every man, woman, and child of Pittsburgh (population 294,860), Allentown (122,623), Erie (94,619), Reading (88,521), Scranton (77,218), Bethlehem (76,370), Harrisburg (49,301), York (44,134), Altoona (43,112), and State College (population 42,216) _**all**_ **winning one-thousand dollars each after taxes!** And this is with only 24.1% of the state's population contributing! The American Stimulus Program can add over **$1.1 billion** to the economy of Pennsylvania each year!

RHODE ISLAND – "The Ocean State"

Odds of Winning in Rhode Island 290 to 1

<u>**WEEKLY DRAWING BASED ON AVERAGE PURCHASE OF $10 (2 TICKETS)**</u>
Participants: 232,072 or 21.9% of the State Population
State Pool: $2,320,720
State & Local Combined Sales Tax (7%): $162,450
Federal ASP Tax (24%): $556,972
Citizens Prize Pool: $1,601,298
WEEKLY DRAWING RESULTS: 1,601 Prizes of $1000 + 1 Mini Prize of $298

<u>**1 YEAR PROJECTION: BASED ON AVERAGE PURCHASE OF 2 TICKETS ($10)**</u>
Rhode Island Annual Revenue: $120,677,440
Rhode Island Annual Tax Revenue: $8,447,400
Annual Federal Tax Revenue: $28,962,544
Annual Winning Tickets of $1000 in Rhode Island: **83,252**
CASH PAID YEARLY TO RHODE ISLANDERS AFTER TAXES: $83,267,496

<u>**COFFEE MILK & GREEN DREAMS!**</u>
Winning tickets awarded to the people of Rhode Island would be the equivalent of every man, woman, and child in Woonsocket (population 41,585), Newport (24,238), Greenville (8,387), and Cumberland Hill (population 8,142) **_all_ winning one-thousand dollars each after taxes!** And this is with only 21.9% of the state's population contributing! The American Stimulus Program can add over **$90,000,000** to the economy of Rhode Island each year!

SOUTH CAROLINA – "The Palmetto State"

Odds of Winning in South Carolina 292 to 1

<u>WEEKLY DRAWING BASED ON AVERAGE PURCHASE OF $10 (2 TICKETS)</u>
Participants: 1,051,513 or 20.4% of the State Population
State Pool: $10,515,130
State & Local Combined Sales Tax (7.46%): $784,428
Federal ASP Tax (24%): $2,523,631
Citizens Prize Pool: $7,207,071
WEEKLY DRAWING RESULTS: 7,207 Prizes of $1000 + 1 Mini Prize of $71

<u>1 YEAR PROJECTION: BASED ON AVERAGE PURCHASE OF 2 TICKETS ($10)</u>
South Carolina Annual Revenue: $546,786,760
South Carolina Annual Tax Revenue: $40,790,256
Annual Federal Tax Revenue: $131,228,812
Annual Winning Tickets of $1000 in South Carolina: **374,764**
CASH PAID YEARLY TO SOUTH CAROLINIANS AFTER TAXES: $374,767,692

<u>IF THE LORD'S WILLIN' AND THE CREEK DON'T RISE!</u>
   Winning tickets awarded to the people of South Carolina would be the equivalent of every man, woman, and child of Charleston (population 138,458), Mount Pleasant (94,932), Summerville (54,198), Myrtle Beach (35,760), Clemson (18,710), Port Royal (13,243), and Garden City (population 10,070) **_all_ winning one-thousand dollars each after taxes!** And this is with only 20.4% of the state's population contributing! The American Stimulus Program can add over **$400,000,000** to the economy of South Carolina each year!

SOUTH DAKOTA – "The Mount Rushmore State"

Odds of Winning in South Carolina 287 to 1

<u>**WEEKLY DRAWING BASED ON AVERAGE PURCHASE OF $10 (2 TICKETS)**</u>

Participants: 185,046 or 20.9% of the State Population

State Pool: $1,850,460

State & Local Combined Sales Tax (6.40%): $118,429

Federal ASP Tax (24%): $444,110

Citizens Prize Pool: $1,287,921

WEEKLY DRAWING RESULTS: 1,287 Prizes of $1000 + 1 Mini Prize of $921

<u>**1 YEAR PROJECTION: BASED ON AVERAGE PURCHASE OF 2 TICKETS ($10)**</u>

South Dakota Annual Revenue: $96,223,920

South Dakota Annual Tax Revenue: $6,158,308

Annual Federal Tax Revenue: $23,093,720

Annual Winning Tickets of $1000 in South Dakota: **66,924**

CASH PAID YEARLY TO SOUTH DAKOTANS AFTER TAXES: $66,971,892

<u>**YOU BETCHA!**</u>

Winning tickets awarded to the people of South Dakota would be the equivalent of every man, woman, and child of Aberdeen (population 29,180), Yankton (14,676), Rapid Valley (9,475), Sturgis (7,287), Belle Fourche (5,538), and Goodwill (population 934) ***all* winning one-thousand dollars each after taxes!** And this is with only 20.9% of the state's population contributing! The American Stimulus Program can add over **$70,000,000** to the economy of South Dakota each year!

TENNESSEE – "The Volunteer State"

Odds of Winning in Tennessee 301 to 1

WEEKLY DRAWING BASED ON AVERAGE PURCHASE OF $10 (2 TICKETS)

Participants: 1,254,013 or 18.4% of the State Population
State Pool: $12,540,130
State & Local Combined Sales Tax (9.53%): $1,195,074
Federal ASP Tax (24%): $3,009,631
Citizens Prize Pool: $8,335,425
WEEKLY DRAWING RESULTS: 8,335 Prizes of $1000 + 1 Mini Prize of $425

1 YEAR PROJECTION: BASED ON AVERAGE PURCHASE OF 2 TICKETS ($10)

Tennessee Annual Revenue: $652,086,760
Tennessee Annual Tax Revenue: $62,143,848
Annual Federal Tax Revenue: $156,500,812
Annual Winning Tickets of $1000 in Tennessee: **443,420**
CASH PAID YEARLY TO TENNESSEANS AFTER TAXES: $433,442,100

WE GOT YOU!

Winning tickets awarded to the people of Tennessee would be the equivalent of every man, woman, and child of Knoxville (population 191,060), Franklin (88,004), Jackson (66,989), Kingsport (56,028), and Germantown (population 38,985) **_all_ winning one-thousand dollars each after taxes!** And this is with only 18.4% of the state's population contributing! The American Stimulus Program can add over **$400,000,000** to the economy of Tennessee each year!

TEXAS – "The Lone Star State"

Odds of Winning in Texas 295 to 1

WEEKLY DRAWING BASED ON AVERAGE PURCHASE OF $10 (2 TICKETS)

Participants: 4,484,613 or 15.5% of the State Population

State Pool: $44,846,130

State & Local Combined Sales Tax (8.19%): $3,672,898

Federal ASP Tax (24%): $10,763,071

Citizens Prize Pool: $30,410,161

WEEKLY DRAWING RESULTS: 30,410 Prizes of $1000 + 1 Mini Prize of $161

1 YEAR PROJECTION: BASED ON AVERAGE PURCHASE OF 2 TICKETS ($10)

Texas Annual Revenue: $2,331,998,760

Texas Annual Tax Revenue: $190,990,696

Annual Federal Tax Revenue: $559,679,692

Annual Winning Tickets of $1000 in Texas: **1,581,320**

CASH PAID YEARLY TO TEXANS AFTER TAXES: $1,581,328,372

EVERYTHING'S BIGGER IN TEXAS!

Winning tickets awarded to the people of Texas would be the equivalent of every man, woman, and child of Austin (population 988,218), Lubbock (260,823), Midland (145,012), Wichita Falls (105,156), Spring (58,756), and Plainview (population 20,024) _**all**_ **winning one-thousand dollars each after taxes!** And this is with only 15.5% of the state's population contributing! The American Stimulus Program can add over **$1.5 billion** to the economy of Texas each year!

UTAH – "The Beehive State"

Odds of Winning in Utah 291 to 1

WEEKLY DRAWING BASED ON AVERAGE PURCHASE OF $10 (2 TICKETS)

Participants: 565,715 or 17.6% of the State Population

State Pool: $5,657,150

State & Local Combined Sales Tax (7.18%): $406,183

Federal ASP Tax (24%): $1,357,716

Citizens Prize Pool: $3,893,251

WEEKLY DRAWING RESULTS: 3,893 Prizes of $1000 + 1 Mini Prize of $251

1 YEAR PROJECTION: BASED ON AVERAGE PURCHASE OF 2 TICKETS ($10)

Utah Annual Revenue: $294,171,800

Utah Annual Tax Revenue: $21,121,516

Annual Federal Tax Revenue: $70,601,232

Annual Winning Tickets of $1000 in Utah: **202,436**

CASH PAID YEARLY TO UTAHNS AFTER TAXES: $202,449,052

YOU BET!

Winning tickets awarded to the people of Utah would be the equivalent of every man, woman, and child of Provo (population 118,592), Logan (52,539), Hurricane (20,181), and Vernal (population 9,744) **_all_ winning one-thousand dollars each after taxes!** And this is with only 17.6% of the state's population contributing! The American Stimulus Program can add over **$200,000,000** to the economy of Utah each year!

VERMONT – "The Green Mountain State"
Odds of Winning in Vermont 286 to 1

<u>WEEKLY DRAWING BASED ON AVERAGE PURCHASE OF $10 (2 TICKETS)</u>
Participants: 157,533 or 25.2% of the State Population
State Pool: $1,575,330
State & Local Combined Sales Tax (6.22%): $97,985
Federal ASP Tax (24%): $378,079
Citizens Prize Pool: $1,099,266
WEEKLY DRAWING RESULTS: 1,099 Prizes of $1000 + 1 Mini Prize of $266

<u>1 YEAR PROJECTION: BASED ON AVERAGE PURCHASE OF 2 TICKETS ($10)</u>
Vermont Annual Revenue: $81,917,160
Vermont Annual Tax Revenue: $5,095,220
Annual Federal Tax Revenue: $19,660,108
Annual Winning Tickets of $1000 in Vermont: **57,148**
CASH PAID YEARLY TO VERMONTERS AFTER TAXES: $57,161,832

<u>JEEZUM CROW!</u>
    Winning tickets awarded to the people of Vermont would be the equivalent of every man, woman, and child of South Burlington (population 20,100), Rutland (15,087), Montpelier (7,356), Newport (4,195), Springfield (4,181), Bellows Falls (2,976), Morrisville (2,040), and Fairfax (population 928) **<u>*all*</u> winning one-thousand dollars each after taxes!** And this is with only 25.2% of the state's population contributing! The American Stimulus Program can add over **$60,000,000** to the economy of Vermont each year!

VIRGINIA – "The Old Dominion"

Odds of Winning in Virginia 284 to 1

WEEKLY DRAWING BASED ON AVERAGE PURCHASE OF $10 (2 TICKETS)

Participants: 1,992,315 or 23.3% of the State Population
State Pool: $19,923,150
State & Local Combined Sales Tax (5.65%): $1,125,657
Federal ASP Tax (24%): $4,781,556
Citizens Prize Pool: $14,015,937
WEEKLY DRAWING RESULTS: 14,015 Prizes of $1000 + 1 Mini Prize of $937

1 YEAR PROJECTION: BASED ON AVERAGE PURCHASE OF 2 TICKETS ($10)

Virginia Annual Revenue: $1,036,003,800
Virginia Annual Tax Revenue: $58,534,164
Annual Federal Tax Revenue: $248,640,912
Annual Winning Tickets of $1000 in Virginia: **728,780**
CASH PAID YEARLY TO VIRGINIANS AFTER TAXES: $728,828,724

BLESS YOUR HEART!

Winning tickets awarded to the people of Virginia would be the equivalent of every man, woman, and child of Chesapeake (population 248,106), Arlington (231,803), Roanoke (99,648), Leesburg (57,029), Charlottesville (49,449), and Danville (population 39,455) **_all_ winning one-thousand dollars each after taxes!** And this is based on only 23.3% of the state's population contributing! The American Stimulus Program can add over **$750,000,000** to the economy of Virginia each year!

WASHINGTON – "The Evergreen State"

Odds of Winning in Washington 299 to 1

<u>WEEKLY DRAWING BASED ON AVERAGE PURCHASE OF $10 (2 TICKETS)</u>

Participants: 1,658,509 or 21.7% of the State Population

State Pool: $16,585,090

State & Local Combined Sales Tax (9.21%): $1,527,486

Federal ASP Tax (24%): $3,980,421

Citizens Prize Pool: $11,077,183

WEEKLY DRAWING RESULTS: 11,077 Prizes of $1000 + 1 Mini Prize of $183

<u>1 YEAR PROJECTION: BASED ON AVERAGE PURCHASE OF 2 TICKETS ($10)</u>

Washington Annual Revenue: $862,424,680

Washington Tax Revenue: $79,429,272

Annual Federal Tax Revenue: $206,981,892

Annual Winning Tickets of $1000 in Washington: **576,004**

CASH PAID YEARLY TO WASHINGTONIANS AFTER TAXES: $576,013,516

<u>TRUE TO THE BLUE!</u>

Winning tickets awarded to the people of Washington would be the equivalent of every man, woman, and child of Spokane (population 223,226), Renton (103,091), Yakima (94,090), Kennewick (86,101), and Richland (population 60,475) **_all_ winning one-thousand dollars each after taxes!** And this is with only 21.7% of the state's population contributing! The American Stimulus Program can add over **$600,000,000** to the economy of Washington each year!

WEST VIRGINIA – "The Mountain State"

Odds of Winning in West Virginia 287 to 1

WEEKLY DRAWING BASED ON AVERAGE PURCHASE OF $10 (2 TICKETS)

Participants: 357,211 or 19.9% of the State Population

State Pool: $3,572,110

State & Local Combined Sales Tax (6.41%): $228,972

Federal ASP Tax (24%): $857,306

Citizens Prize Pool: $2,485,832

WEEKLY DRAWING RESULTS: 2,485 Prizes of $1000 + 1 Mini Prize of $832

1 YEAR PROJECTION: BASED ON AVERAGE PURCHASE OF 2 TICKETS ($10)

West Virginia Annual Revenue: $185,749,720

West Virginia Tax Revenue: $11,906,544

Annual Federal Tax Revenue: $44,579,912

Annual Winning Tickets of $1000 in West Virginia: **129,220**

CASH PAID YEARLY TO WEST VIRGINIANS AFTER TAXES: $129,263,264

PUT IT IN THE POKE!

Winning tickets awarded to the people of West Virginia would be the equivalent of every man, woman, and child of Charleston (population 45,703), Wheeling (25,941), Fairmont (18,349), Beckley (15,547), Vienna (10,018), Oak Hill (7,954), and Grafton (population 4,978) **_all_ winning one-thousand dollars each after taxes!** And this is with only 19.9% of the state's population contributing! The American Stimulus Program can add over **$130,000,000** to the economy of West Virginia each year!

WISCONSIN – "The Badger State"

Odds of Winning in Wisconsin 284 to 1

<u>WEEKLY DRAWING BASED ON AVERAGE PURCHASE OF $10 (2 TICKETS)</u>
Participants: 1,488,075 or 25.5% of the State Population
State Pool: $14,880,750
State & Local Combined Sales Tax (5.46%): $812,488
Federal ASP Tax (24%): $3,571,380
Citizens Prize Pool: $10,496,882
WEEKLY DRAWING RESULTS: 10,496 Prizes of $1000 + 1 Mini Prize of $882

<u>1 YEAR PROJECTION: BASED ON AVERAGE PURCHASE OF 2 TICKETS ($10)</u>
Wisconsin Annual Revenue: $773,799,000
Wisconsin Annual Tax Revenue: $42,249,376
Annual Federal Tax Revenue: $185,711,760
Annual Winning Tickets of $1000 in Wisconsin: **545,792**
CASH PAID YEARLY TO CHEESEHEADS AFTER TAXES: $545,837,864

<u>AW GEEZ!</u>
Winning tickets awarded to the people of Wisconsin would be the equivalent of every man, woman, and child of Madison (population 264,030), Green Bay (105,413), Oshkosh (66,831), Wausau (38,532), Mount Pleasant (27,310), Fox Crossing (19,109), and Bellevue (population 15,935) **_all_ winning one-thousand dollars each after taxes!** And this is with only 25.5% of the state's population contributing! The American Stimulus Program can add over **$600,000,000** to the economy of Wisconsin each year!

WYOMING – "The Equality State"

Odds of Winning in Wyoming 283 to 1

WEEKLY DRAWING BASED ON AVERAGE PURCHASE OF $10 (2 TICKETS)

Participants: 127,924 or 22.1% of the State Population
State Pool: $1,279,240
State & Local Combined Sales Tax (5.34%): $68,311
Federal ASP Tax (24%): $307,017
Citizens Prize Pool: $903,912
WEEKLY DRAWING RESULTS: 903 Prizes of $1000 + 1 Mini Prize of $912

1 YEAR PROJECTION: BASED ON AVERAGE PURCHASE OF 2 TICKETS ($10)

Wyoming Annual Revenue: $66,520,480
Wyoming Annual Tax Revenue: $3,552,193
Annual Federal Tax Revenue: $15,964,884
Annual Winning Tickets of $1000 in Wyoming: **46,956**
CASH PAID YEARLY TO WYOMINGITES AFTER TAXES: $47,003,424

COWBOY UP!

Winning tickets awarded to the people of Wyoming would be the equivalent of every man, woman, and child of Rock Springs (population 22,272), Torrington (6,793), Douglas (5,945), Buffalo (4,545), Mills (3,937), and Newcastle (population 3,184), **_all_ winning one-thousand dollars each after taxes!** And this is with only 22.1% of the state's population contributing! The American Stimulus Program can add over **$50,000,000** to the economy of Wyoming each year!

<u>Annual Statistics of the</u>
<u>American Stimulus Program Simulation</u>

<u>CASH</u> Amount Paid Out to Americans <u>**AFTER**</u> Taxes
$24 Billion! ($24,346,904,400)

Annual Federal Tax Revenue Collected
$8.5 Billion! ($8,508,728,511)

Annual State & Local Tax Revenue Collected
$2.5 Billion! ($2,541,177,891)

<u>Adjusting the Citizens Prize Pool</u>

There may be times when it becomes necessary to modify the Citizens Prize Pool payouts to dramatically increase the number of winning tickets. Suppose a State cannot produce adequate participation because it has been adversely affected by an economic, social, or medical crisis. In that case, the ASP can increase the number of winning tickets by reducing the main cash prize. The expansion of winning tickets will provide a wider spread of stimulus but at a decreased fiscal amount. For example, the ASP can double the number of winning tickets by reducing the principal prize amount from $1000 to $500. Nationally, this would mean the prize pool of winning tickets would increase from 460,000 to 920,000 per week. Although the ASP ideally provides cash prizes that match our national average weekly earnings, there may be times when changing a State's prize payout may be necessary. We can use this adjustment to help alleviate a crisis. We can also increase the number of winning tickets for times of National celebration!

Flexibility & Fun

Although our simulation uses $1000 as the primary prize, we can adjust that for National Holidays and events of American significance. Here is a list of suggested prize changes for special events in 2021!

Independence Day Celebration Cash on July 4th, 2021

A July 4th special payout of $300 would increase nationwide prizes from 460,000 to over 1.5 million winning tickets!

Back to School Shopping Cash Drawing on August 8th, 2021

A Going Back to School special payout of $400 would increase nationwide prizes from 460,000 to 1.1 million winning tickets!

Christmas Cash for Black Friday, November 26th, 2021

Drawing Date: November 21st, 2021

A special Christmas Shopping payout of $500 would increase the nationwide prizes from 460,000 to 920,000 winning tickets!

New Year's Eve Celebration Cash for December 31st, 2021

Drawing Date: December 26th, 2021

A New Year's special payout of $200 would increase the nationwide number of prizes from 460,000 to 2.3 million winning tickets!

Pro Football's Championship Game Party Cash on February 6th, 2022

A Football viewing party cash award amount of $250 would increase nationwide prizes from 460,000 to over 1.8 million winning tickets!

Public Relations

The American Stimulus Program may prove to be one of the most successful public relations vehicles between the Government and the American people ever devised. The weekly drawings could provide a unique opportunity for the Federal Government to recognize American excellence. With a collective audience nearing 66,000,000 viewers, each drawing would allow the acknowledgment of the best people America has to offer. Envision a simple but powerful live streaming production that captivates a national audience watching as their state maps light up with the cities and towns where winning citizens reside.

As the weekly drawings unfold, we can celebrate Americans for their service to our country. Each week we can collectively praise our frontline healthcare workers, first responders, medical heroes, peace officers, teachers, and soldiers, just to name a few. With fitting musical accompaniment and engaging visuals flashing across their state map, the drawings will become an event that is entertaining, emotional, and exciting.

Imagine a tribute to our War Veterans accompanied by the music of Bruce Springsteen's "Born in the USA." Or perhaps a drawing devoted to our proud Immigrant population with Neil Diamond's "Coming to America" ringing out as hundreds of thousands of Americans celebrate their good new fortune.

The drawings will be short and sweet, usually lasting less than ten minutes. The ASP will draw the tickets at a lightning pace, winning Americans will be alerted on their devices, and the Federal Government can show their appreciation to our citizens. We can all enjoy some of the most iconic music as we eagerly watch to see if we have won. The American Stimulus Program may prove to be the best ten minutes of entertainment each week!

<u>War!</u>

On January 20th, 2020, the first patient was diagnosed with the coronavirus in Washington. In less than one year, we have incurred nearly 400,000 deaths across the United States. We have failed to manage the spread and prevention of this virus.

The Federal Reserve has distributed over 3.2 trillion dollars to support households, state and local governments, employers, and financial markets. They have issued near-zero interest rates and provided forward guidance. They backstopped money market mutual funds. They have encouraged banks to lend and supported loans to small and mid-sized businesses. They also extended loans to nonprofit institutions, supported state and municipal borrowing and other aid as well.

By January 2021, thousands were still dying daily, and over 11 million Americans were unemployed. In less than 12 months, a virus had done to the United States what no foreign power had ever achieved through war. We face an invisible enemy that destroys jobs, businesses, families, lives, and our future. Please make no mistake about it. We are at war!

We are awaiting the national vaccination of the United States. From where we stand now, looking to the future, we have millions of Americans struggling to cope with what tomorrow may bring. 30 to 40 million Americans face the risk of eviction, and nearly 26 million households do not have enough food. We are living with uncertainty in every aspect of our lives. Americans are anxious, angry, depressed, stressed, and even suicidal. We are at war!

We watch as our leaders put together another stimulus package to carry the U.S. economy temporarily. Our state and local governments are broke or damn near to it. The Federal Reserve keeps printing money to prop us up. We realize that this type of artificial stimulus will inevitably lead to a tidal wave of taxes and restrictions, suppressing economic growth. Again, we are at war!

We are fighting back, but a real economic rebound is going to take time. And whether we want to admit it or not, many of the jobs we closed will just not be coming back. We have no idea how millions of unemployed Americans will find future employment. We faced a similar situation in the past. In 1933, during the Great Depression, the New Deal activated a myriad of work programs. It put America back to work and may have saved capitalism. But unlike the New Deal legislation of the 1930s, work programs will not help us until our workforce is vaccinated and can work safely against our enemy, Covid-19.

The American Stimulus Program responds directly to our consumer spending drought. The ASP will put forth cash to a country that may not return to work for the foreseeable future. Many may not be able to work a 40-hour workweek, but money in the hands of hundreds of thousands of Americans every seven days will affect our economy as if they did! The ASP can help us win this war against our unseen enemy. It can create income, pay taxes, and restore our economy week by week, *five dollars at a time*.

Let us go to war!

Dear Mr. President

Our President is facing many problems with Covid-19 and all the residual issues stemming from its destructive impact. Here is an open letter to request a review by his administration concerning the American Stimulus Program.

Dear Mr. President,

Congratulations on your November victory! I am writing you this letter to introduce the American Stimulus Program. It is an economic tool to stimulate consumer spending, raise state and local tax revenue, and replenish and grow federal tax dollars. It is a genuinely nonpartisan instrument whose primary objective is to get cash to our citizens every week.

As you know, Americans are hurting in many ways, and your administration is facing many nationwide fiscal challenges. Challenges that cannot be solved alone through intermittent federal stimulus packages. We now owe more than we are worth better than 100% of our outstanding assets in the United States. The American Stimulus Program provides an alternative to increasing our national debt.

The ASP will provide our citizens in every state with cash every seven days from monies voluntarily procured by our fellow Americans. I ask that your administration expediently review its content. They will find a straightforward approach to provide our population with financial relief and incrementally boost consumer spending. We need your help to give the American people the online infrastructure to invest in themselves. The ASP is an economic implement that can supply real, tangible results that will positively define your administration's financial performance.

I have concluded a full simulation of the American Stimulus Program. It produced an annual return of over 24 billion dollars paid out to over 24,000,000 Americans _after_ taxes! The ASP also made over 8.5 billion dollars in federal tax revenue and over 2.5 billion dollars in state and local tax dollars. Incredibly, this can be accomplished with only slightly more than 20% of our population participating.

Americans want to work! We want our lives back! But currently, we are at the mercy of the devastation caused by the coronavirus. The ASP can provide the U.S. with an economic advantage now and post Covid-19 in our extremely competitive world. This Program has its place in any economic cycle, whether it be depression, recession, recovery, or expansion. Please review the American Stimulus Program with the sense of urgency, practicality, and focus that the American people deserve. It may very well be the most crucial fiscal legislation for our country at this critical time.

With Much Appreciation,

Michael Palser

Creator, Designer, Author, and Enthusiast

American Stimulus Program

<u>True Nonpartisan Legislation</u>

We are so very divided in this country. We have split ourselves up into three different camps. We are on the red team, the blue team, or we are indifferent. The American Stimulus Program has no political ties. It does not earmark any tax dollars collected for any other government programs. It does not set aside one single dollar for the Wall on the southern border. It does not set aside one single dollar for the Green New Deal.

No tax dollars will be earmarked or committed to any other government programs before any weekly drawing. The decisions on how to spend those collected tax dollars will be determined after collection and not before! We need to ensure that our tax dollars are being committed to our most immediate needs at the time and that no political biases or other programs interfere with the implementation of the American Stimulus Program. We will let Congress decide those needs after-tax monies are collected. After all, that is why we pay them.

We can all see the pain in our communities. We all understand that this virus is crippling our fellow citizens in lots of different ways. Yet, we cannot understand how our current Congress has been reluctant to pass stimulus packages while we suffer. The reality is that they just do not possess the proper tool to do their job. This Program ensures stimulus each week effectively, efficiently, and without political hesitation. The American Stimulus Program will ease the financial and political indecision during Covid-19 and for any threat in our future.

The ASP will prove to be a vital economic tool. It will be a crucial asset during times of economic expansion, peak, contraction, or trough. It will jumpstart our economy ahead of other countries like China, Russia, and Japan. It will give us a competitive advantage now and post Covid-19. Unfortunately, with their open disregard for intellectual property, other countries will copy and produce their versions of the American Stimulus Program based on their economic situations. But we can get there first!

We cannot let any of our political differences stand in the way of the Program's honest intentions. We need the U.S. government to provide the online infrastructure for the American Stimulus Program. It is crucial for Congress and the United States President to work in unison to provide a genuinely nonpartisan bill for the American people now!

Attention Legislators!

Examine, explore, and evaluate the objectives of this economic tool closely. You will find that it can become a cornerstone of our future financial success. Whether we are in rough waters or enjoying smooth sailing, the American Stimulus Program has a place in all economic conditions in all fifty states!

Attention Americans!

Please take the time to contact your local and state representatives to express your support for the American Stimulus Program!

Behind the Curtain

With social media platforms like Facebook, YouTube, Reddit, Twitter, Instagram, Parler, and TikTok, amongst others, we have become the most well-documented generation in the history of the world. We can reach out and express ourselves to many people with the single push of a button. I submit that after this Program gets off the ground, we will see and hear many stories about how the American Stimulus Program has impacted our lives.

Some may ridicule the top prize of one-thousand dollars as not being enough to help. However, with many of our fellow citizens struggling from day-to-day, this modest monetary boost may make all the difference in the world. When we get a peek behind the curtain, we will learn how a mere thousand dollars allowed a single mother to feed her children and reestablish calm and normality back into their lives. We will witness the stories of how one thousand dollars kept good people from becoming homeless. Or how an investment of five dollars allowed someone to get medical attention or medications they so desperately needed. Or how one thousand dollars tipped back the scales of depression and saved someone from committing a crime or even suicide because they had no one to turn to in a time of desperation.

There is a whole underbelly of our society to be exposed because of this Program. But I believe the most reoccurring theme will be how winning a paltry thousand dollars prevented someone from feeling helpless, forgotten, discarded, and frankly invisible in the most powerful country in the world. *Restored confidence and hope can come from many sources.* The American Stimulus Program will reveal itself to be one of those sources.

Americans are about to learn how a little can go a long way. I know that sounds dramatic but just watch our social media platforms after each drawing. Our stories will surprise, stimulate, and inspire us all to be a little more patient and a bit more understanding of one another.

And that is a good thing!

Our Best Days Are Ahead of Us

The day will come when our country resembles life as it was back in 2019. Americans will be returning to work, our children will be physically back in school, and we will go out into public without face masks. We will be able to interact with our family and friends without socially distancing. When that time comes, the ASP will keep doing its job.

The American Stimulus Program will keep providing state and local tax revenue, producing federal tax dollars, and enriching Americans with cash every week. Although the ASP will continue to work for us, its role will change when we have moved past the coronavirus. Instead of being an economic tool to lean on during difficult times, it will transform into a backstop ready to defend the United States against the next national crisis.

When that day comes, we will be living in rarified times. We will begin to progress into a new climate of confidence and wealth. We will have created a consumer spending stimulus tool to help us and to insure ourselves against the unexpected. We will have rediscovered that by collectively working together against any enemy, we are unstoppable. Whether it is a foreign adversary, a medical or technological virus, or some unknown menace, America will endure. *We shall adapt, overcome, and we shall prosper.*

So, enjoy your life.

The American Stimulus Program will have your back!